SCHOLASTIC
READ & RESPOND

Bringing the best books to life in the classroom

Activities based on
Hetty Feather
By Jacqueline Wilson

Recommended system requirements:
Windows: XP (Service Pack 3), Vista (Service Pack 2), Windows 7 or Windows 8 with 2.33GHz processor
Mac: OS 10.6 to 10.8 with Intel Core™ Duo processor
1GB RAM (recommended)
1024 x 768 Screen resolution
CD-ROM drive (24x speed recommended)
Adobe Reader (version 9 recommended for Mac users)
Broadband internet connections (for installation and updates)

For all technical support queries (including no CD drive), please phone Scholastic Customer Services on 0845 6039091.

Designed using Adobe Indesign
Published by Scholastic Education, an imprint of Scholastic Ltd
Book End, Range Road, Witney, Oxfordshire, OX29 0YD
Registered office: Westfield Road, Southam,
Warwickshire CV47 0RA
www.scholastic.co.uk

Printed and bound by Ashford Colour Press
© 2016 Scholastic Ltd
1 2 3 4 5 6 7 8 9   6 7 8 9 0 1 2 3 4 5

British Library Cataloguing-in-Publication Data
A catalogue record for this book is available from the British Library.
ISBN 978-1407-15877-8

Due to the nature of the web, we cannot guarantee the content or links of any site mentioned. We strongly recommend that teachers check websites before using them in the classroom.

Author Eileen Jones
Editorial team Rachel Morgan, Jenny Wilcox, Becky Breuer, Caroline Low, Jo Kemp, Elizabeth Evans
Series designer Neil Salt
Designer Anna Oliwa
Illustrator Simon Walmesley
Digital development Hannah Barnett, Phil Crothers and MWA Technologies Private Ltd

Acknowledgements
The publishers gratefully acknowledge permission to reproduce the following copyright material:
David Higham Associates for the use of extracts from *Hetty Feather* by Jacqueline Wilson. Text © 2009, Jacqueline Wilson. (2009, Random House Children's Books). **Random House Children's Publishers UK** for the use of the cover from *Hetty Feather* by Jacqueline Wilson and illustrated by Nick Sharratt. Text © 2009, Jacqueline Wilson. Illustrations © 2009, Nick Sharratt. (2009, Random House Children's Publishers UK).

Every effort has been made to trace copyright holders for the works reproduced in this book, and the publishers apologise for any inadvertent omissions.

CONTENTS

INTRODUCTION

Read & Respond provides teaching ideas related to a specific children's book. The series focuses on best-loved books and brings you ways to use them to engage your class and enthuse them about reading.

The book is divided into different sections:

- **About the book and author:** gives you some background information about the book and the author.

- **Guided reading:** breaks the book down into sections and gives notes for using it with guided reading groups. A bookmark has been provided on page 10 containing comprehension questions. The children can be directed to refer to these as they read.

- **Shared reading:** provides extracts from the children's books with associated notes for focused work. There is also one non-fiction extract that relates to the children's book.

- **Grammar, punctuation & spelling:** provides word-level work related to the children's book so you can teach grammar, punctuation and spelling in context.

- **Plot, character & setting:** contains activity ideas focused on the plot, characters and the setting of the story.

- **Talk about it:** has speaking and listening activities related to the children's book. These activities may be based directly on the children's book or be broadly based on the themes and concepts of the story.

- **Get writing:** provides writing activities related to the children's book. These activities may be based directly on the children's book or be broadly based on the themes and concepts of the story.

- **Assessment:** contains short activities that will help you assess whether the children have understood concepts and curriculum objectives. They are designed to be informal activities to feed into your planning.

The activities follow the same format:

- **Objective:** the objective for the lesson. It will be based upon a curriculum objective, but will often be more specific to the focus being covered.

- **What you need:** a list of resources you need to teach the lesson, including digital resources (printable pages, interactive activities and media resources, see page 5).

- **What to do:** the activity notes.

- **Differentiation:** this is provided where specific and useful differentiation advice can be given to support and/or extend the learning in the activity. Differentiation by providing additional adult support has not been included as this will be at a teacher's discretion based upon specific children's needs and ability, as well as the availability of support.

The activities are numbered for reference within each section and should move through the text sequentially – so you can use the lesson while you are reading the book. Once you have read the book, most of the activities can be used in any order you wish.

Below are brief guidance notes for using the CD-ROM. For more detailed information, please click on the '?' button in the top right-hand corner of the screen.

The program contains the following:
- the extract pages from the book
- all of the photocopiable pages from the book
- additional printable pages
- interactive on-screen activities
- media resources.

Getting started

Put the CD-ROM into your CD-ROM drive. If you do not have a CD-ROM drive, phone Scholastic Customer Services on 0845 6039091.

- For Windows users, the install wizard should autorun, if it fails to do so then navigate to your CD-ROM drive. Then follow the installation process.
- For Mac users, copy the disk image file to your hard drive. After it has finished copying double click it to mount the disk image. Navigate to the mounted disk image and run the installer. After installation the disk image can be unmounted and the DMG can be deleted from the hard drive.
- To install on a network, see the ReadMe file located on the CD-ROM (navigate to your drive).

To complete the installation of the program you need to open the program and click 'Update' in the pop-up. Please note – this CD-ROM is web-enabled and the content will be downloaded from the internet to your hard drive to populate the CD-ROM with the relevant resources. This only needs to be done on first use, after this you will be able to use the CD-ROM without an internet connection. If at any point any content is updated, you will receive another pop-up upon start up when there is an internet connection.

Main menu

The main menu is the first screen that appears. Here you can access: terms and conditions, registration links, how to use the CD-ROM and credits. To access a specific book click on the relevant button (NB only titles installed will be available). You can filter by the

drop-down lists if you wish. You can search all resources by clicking 'Search' in the bottom left-hand corner. You can also log in and access favourites that you have bookmarked.

Resources

By clicking on a book on the Main menu, you are taken to the resources for that title. The resources are: Media, Interactives, Extracts and Printables. Select the category and then launch a resource by clicking the play button.

Teacher settings

In the top right-hand corner of the screen is a small 'T' icon. This is the teacher settings area. It is password protected, the password is: login. This area will allow you to choose the print quality settings for interactive activities ('Default' or 'Best') and also allow you to check for updates to the program or re-download all content to the disk via Refresh all content. You can also set up user logins so that you can save and access favourites. Once a user is set up, they can enter by clicking the login link underneath the 'T' and '?' buttons.

Search

You can access an all resources search by clicking the search button on the bottom left of the Main menu. You can search for activities by type (using the drop-down filter) or by keyword by typing into the box. You can then assign resources to your favourites area or launch them directly from the search area.

CURRICULUM LINKS

Section	Activity	Curriculum objectives
Guided reading		Comprehension: To ask questions to improve their understanding of a text.
Shared reading	1	Comprehension: To participate in discussion about both books that are read to them and those they can read for themselves, taking turns and listening to what others say.
	2	Comprehension: To draw inferences such as inferring characters' feelings, thoughts and motives from their actions, and justifying inferences with evidence.
	3	Comprehension: To discuss and evaluate how authors use language, including figurative language, considering the impact on the reader.
	4	Comprehension: To read books that are structured in different ways and reading for a range of purposes.
Grammar, punctuation & spelling	1	Composition: To use fronted adverbials.
	2	Composition: To extend the range of sentences with more than one clause by using a wider range of conjunctions.
	3	Composition: To use direct speech.
	4	Composition: To use and punctuate direct speech.
	5	Transcription: To use further prefixes and understand how to add them.
	6	Transcription: To spell further homophones.
Plot, character & setting	1	Comprehension: To predict what might happen from details stated and implied.
	2	Comprehension: To draw inferences and justify inferences with evidence.
	3	Comprehension: To infer characters' feelings from their actions.
	4	Comprehension: To ask questions to improve their understanding of a text.
	5	Comprehension: To use dictionaries to check the meanings of words that they have read.
	6	Comprehension: To identify themes in a wide range of books.
	7	Comprehension: To ask questions to improve their understanding of a text.
	8	Comprehension: To read books that are structured in different ways.

Section	Activity	Curriculum objectives
Talk about it	1	Spoken language: To participate in role play.
	2	Spoken language: To use spoken language to develop understanding through speculating, hypothesising, imagining and exploring ideas.
	3	Spoken language: To give well-structured narratives for different purposes, including for expressing feelings.
	4	Spoken language: To use spoken language to develop understanding through speculating, hypothesising, imagining and exploring ideas.
	5	Spoken language: To participate in discussions and debates.
	6	Spoken language: To maintain attention and participate actively in collaborative conversations, staying on topic and initiating and responding to comments.
Get writing	1	Composition: To choose pronouns appropriately for clarity and cohesion and to avoid repetition.
	2	Composition: To write non-narrative material, using simple organisational devices.
	3	Composition: To assess the effectiveness of their own and others' writing.
	4	Composition: To plan their writing by discussing and recording ideas.
	5	Composition: To draft a narrative, creating settings, characters and plot.
	6	Composition: To compose and rehearse sentences orally before writing a text.
Assessment	1	Comprehension: To explain the meaning of words in context.
	2	Composition: To indicate possession by using the possessive apostrophe with plural nouns.
	3	Composition: To plan their writing by discussing and recording ideas.
	4	Comprehension: To identify themes in a wide range of books.
	5	Comprehension: To retrieve and record information from non-fiction.
	6	Composition: To draft and write non-narrative material, using simple organisational devices.

HETTY FEATHER

About the book

Hetty Feather is a wonderful book for Key Stage 2 study. Gripping, heart-rending, exciting and frightening, it is a compelling read from a leading children's author of our time. It extends across the curriculum with its strong basis of historical and geographical truth. The main character is Hetty Feather, a foundling girl at London's Victorian Foundling Hospital. She is fictional, but her experiences, environment and meagre possessions mirror Victorian reality. Hetty, now aged ten, tells her life story. Her experiences may seem overwhelming, but Hetty soon shows herself to be a feisty character who teaches the reader the importance of courage, determination and perseverance.

From the beginning, Hetty wins the reader's support and empathy. As a baby, given up by her destitute mother, Hetty becomes the property of the Foundling Hospital. She is dispatched to a rural foster family for five years, where she enjoys a happy life and forms close bonds with her carers. However, Hetty has a strong imagination and a sneaked trip to the circus results in an encounter with a glamorous circus performer. Could this be Hetty's real mother? This search for the mother who had to give her up is a major theme of the story. The book tracks that search through Hetty's next five years of institution life at the Foundling Hospital. Life is harder here, but Hetty remains a spirited adventurer, speaking up for a friend, defying authority, and risking punishment to see her blood brother. Throughout her journey through institution life, she remains determined to keep her individual personality, to better herself and to stay Hetty Feather.

About the author

Jacqueline Wilson was born in Bath in 1945 and grew up in Kingston-on-Thames, where she still lives today. She has written many books for children, and her sensitive understanding of the way children live and the problems they encounter, together with her sense of humour, have made her an extremely popular author. She has sold millions of books – her total stands at more than 20 million in the UK alone. In June 2002 Jacqueline was given an OBE for services to literacy in schools and was made a Dame in the New Year's Honours List for 2008. She was Children's Laureate from 2005 to 2007.

Key facts

Hetty Feather
Author: Jacqueline Wilson
Illustrator: Nick Sharratt
First published: 2009 by Random House Children's Books
Did you know: Jacqueline Wilson's work has been on countless shortlists and has won many awards, including the Smarties Prize and the Children's Book Award. *The Illustrated Mum* won the Guardian Children's Fiction Award and the 1999 Children's Book of the Year at the British Book Awards. It was also shortlisted for the 1999 Whitbread Children's Book Award. *The Story of Tracy Beaker* won the 2002 Blue Peter People's Choice Award. Jacqueline Wilson was appointed the fourth Children's Laureate in 2005.

Chapter 1

Discuss question 12 on the Guided Reading bookmark (page 12). Confirm an opening's function: to hook the reader. Comment on: first person writing through the title character; Victorian setting and vocabulary ('cab', 'gaslight'); unfamiliar characters ('Jem'); and the 'conversation' between the two babies. Suggest that the reader is intrigued, and responds to Hetty's friendly writing voice ('Don't mock.'). Assess the chapter's success. Is the threat of 'the great chill baby hospital' a final hook?

Chapter 2

Explain 'fostered foundlings' (abandoned babies). Comment on Hetty's attitude to Jem ('my heart thumped with love for him') and her reluctance to share their squirrel-house game. Why is Gideon an exception? (He is her 'special little basket brother'.) Discuss questions 1 and 2 on the Guided Reading bookmark.

Chapter 3

Read Jem's account of school. Are today's schoolchildren punished for confusing letters? What does the reader know of Hetty's personality? (daring, mischievous, caring) What word is used for Hetty's imaginative skills? ('picturing') Discuss question 8 on the Guided Reading bookmark. Consider the family's reaction to Martha's departure and their attitude to the Foundling Hospital.

Chapter 4

Discuss question 5 on the Guided Reading bookmark. Ask: *How does Hetty react to the new baby?* Discuss her jealous need for Jem's attention. Highlight the reference to Mother's payment. Does Hetty understand? Why do Mother and Jem favour Saul? How does Hetty feel when Saul goes? (sad,

and guilty for not being a good sister) Let the children re-read Father's explanation of fostering. What shows Hetty's limited understanding? (She fears being eaten.) How does she think she will escape staying at the Foundling Hospital? (by being 'so bad')

Chapter 5

Discuss question 5 on the Guided Reading bookmark. Comment on Hetty's constant questions and Mother's reluctance to answer them. How does Hetty feel when told 'You belong to the Foundling Hospital'? Why does Jem make promises about their future? Are they genuine? Pick out 'loomed': it suits Hetty's negative thoughts. Consider Hetty's strong personality and her determination to keep a secret.

Chapter 6

Examine the vivid description of the circus acts. Discuss question 9 on the Guided Reading bookmark. Remind the children that Hetty is the storyteller. Ask: *Are her circus memories unusually strong?* Remind them of Hetty's age; she does not have much longer with Mother. What makes Hetty so attached to Madame Adeline? (the words 'my Little Star') Do the children think that Hetty will forget her quickly? Which of Nat's words frightens Jem? ('three') Why?

Chapter 7

Suggest that Mother and Father react to Gideon's disappearance as if he were their own child. Consider Hetty's reaction. Discuss question 10 on the Guided Reading bookmark. Does Hetty think selfishly of life with Madame Adeline? Re-read the final five paragraphs. How is Hetty disappointed? What does she believe? (Madame Adeline is her real mother.) Is this true?

Chapter 8

Discuss the effects on Gideon of going missing. What is the worst? (He stops talking.) What makes Hetty realise that she and Gideon are about to leave? (Mother boils water to bath them.) Examine Jem and Hetty's bond: her need for him; his patience with her picturing; his generous gift. Point out Sam's comments in the final pages. Ask: *Does Gideon understand what is happening? What does Hetty feel?*

Chapter 9

Explain the kiss simile 'like a little caged bird'. Ask: *Does Hetty's imagining skill comfort her?* Point out Hetty's 'No!' in answer to the question about her mother. What does this reveal? (her belief in finding her mother) Ask: *Are the lockets special presents?* (They are engraved with the children's numbers.) *Where could Mother have got them?* (They were perhaps given by the hospital.) Suggest that the author includes London place names for historical authenticity. Discuss questions 5 and 12 on the Guided Reading bookmark.

Chapter 10

This is an important point in the story: Hetty returns to the Foundling School. Why does Mother run? What reveals her distress? (her hand over her eyes) Investigate Hetty's harsh treatment (for example, unsmiling nurse; scrubbed 'viciously'; hair shorn). Identify Hetty's argumentativeness, determination and quick-thinking resourcefulness (hiding the sixpence). Ask: *Is it cruel to take her rag baby?* Let the children re-read the final paragraph. What is Hetty determined to do? (be true to herself) Discuss question 6 on the Guided Reading bookmark.

Chapter 11

Who shows Hetty 'unexpected kindness'? (Ida) How? Discuss Hetty's fight with Sheila. Ask: *Was she wise not to name her attacker? How does Hetty manage to visit Gideon?* Point out that Gideon 'hung his head' when asked about other boys. Why? Ask: *What does Hetty seem to enjoy most about her meeting with Gideon? What is wonderful about the way the visit ends?* (Gideon speaks.)

Chapter 12

Debate why Ida is so friendly. Talk about the hospital regime and punishments. Why do the Sunday visitors come? (perhaps as an act of charity) What does Hetty think? (One could be Madame Adeline.) Discuss Hetty's love of reading and writing stories. Ask: *Can Ida read? Do the newspaper stories help Hetty?* (She uses them to entertain and frighten.) *Who becomes Hetty's friend?* Discuss question 5 on the Guided Reading bookmark.

Chapter 13

Explore Hetty's feelings and her awareness of others' feelings. Consider how Hetty dreads losing Polly's friendship, and how Polly's note reassures her. Ask: *What does Hetty enjoy about being 'sorely ill'? Why does she blush when she thinks of Ida's feelings? How does she react when she recognises the sick Saul? Does Hetty care about Saul's death?* Discuss question 6 on the Guided Reading bookmark.

Chapter 14

Consider why Hetty and Polly are Miss Newman's favourites. Ask: *Is Hetty selfish not to invite Sheila to walk with Polly and her? Is Hetty wrong to take the lavender and apron? Why does Ida cry when she receives the present? How is Ida's present to Hetty thoughtful?* (It is small enough to hide.) Point out 'proudly', showing Hetty's sisterly feelings. Why is she 'relieved'? (Gideon is doing well.) Ask: *Does Polly enjoy this Christmas? How?*

Chapter 15
Point out the quick passage of time and changes: Hetty dislikes her new teacher and is discouraged from demonstrating intelligence. What skills are now being taught to Hetty? (washing clothes and scrubbing floors) What is she being prepared for? (being a servant) Discuss Polly and Hetty's punishments. Ask: *Would such things happen today? What helps Hetty through the terrible night?* (Ida keeps guard.) *Does the punishment teach Hetty respect for Matron Bottomly and Miss Morley?*

Chapter 16
Discuss Hetty's encounters with Gideon. Point out 'as if I was embracing a stranger', 'politely' and 'at a loss for further conversation'. What has happened to their relationship? Consider Polly's move. Is she 'fortunate'? Should her new parents change her name? Who comforts Hetty after Polly's departure? (Ida and Eliza) What distresses her? (Jem has played and planned the same things with Eliza.) Re-read the final paragraph. How does Hetty see her future?

Chapter 17
Point out 'wounded'. Ask: *Does Hetty intend hurting Ida? How?* Discuss Ida's view that Hetty should know her place. Point out Ida's comment about the workhouse, a reminder of the shame attached. What could be Ida's reason for choosing Sheila? Explain the rarity of a royal jubilee. In London, why does Hetty think of Polly? (She feels alone.) Why is she particularly pleased to meet Gideon? (He comes to find her.) Are the children surprised that Hetty still hopes to join the circus?

Chapter 18
Contrast Hetty's courage with Gideon's timidity. Ask: *Is Hetty foolish to search for the circus?* Identify deviousness (changing direction while someone watches); endurance (walking for over half an hour to the first circus); and perseverance (finding Hampstead Heath). What does Hetty hope will happen when she finds Madame Adeline? (She will live with her.) Who is the old lady in the wagon? (Madame Adeline) Does she really remember Hetty? (No, she is protecting her feelings.) How does the chapter end?

Chapter 19
Ask: *Does Hetty become cheerful when she talks to herself about being as free as the air?* Discuss question 11 on the Guided Reading bookmark. Suggest that Hetty finds it harder now to comfort herself by 'picturing'. Why? (She is older and in more difficult situations.) Why is Rosabel warned not to let street children near her? (Her parents probably fear germs.) Who comes to Hetty's rescue? (Sissy, the flower-seller). Ask: *What will happen next?*

Chapter 20
Discuss question 12 on the Guided Reading bookmark. Emphasise tying up loose ends and resolving earlier questions, for example, who the attentive Sunday visitor is, and why Ida fusses over Hetty. Discuss question 1 on the Guided Reading bookmark. Debate Miss Smith's opinion that the Foundling Hospital is 'an excellent institution in most respects'. Could the school be improved? Ask: *Does the chapter end well? Why? Do you wonder about Hetty's future?* Suggest that the author allows for a sequel.

■ SCHOLASTIC
READ & RESPOND
Bringing the best books to life in the classroom

Hetty Feather
by Jacqueline Wilson

Focus on...
Meaning

1. In *Hetty Feather*, do you think Hetty and the other foundlings are being looked after carelessly or well? Supply evidence for your answer.

2. What does Hetty know about her mother? What has she imagined?

3. What predictions can you make about what may happen later in *Hetty Feather* from the way the chapter ends?

4. Does Hetty have any friends? Explain why it is important to Hetty to have a special friend of her own. What does this suggest about Hetty?

Focus on...
Organisation

5. Do you think the author uses speech effectively in *Hetty Feather*? Give an example and explain how it adds to the story.

6. How does the author build up atmosphere and information about the characters in this chapter?

■ SCHOLASTIC
READ & RESPOND
Bringing the best books to life in the classroom

Hetty Feather
by Jacqueline Wilson

Focus on...
Language and features

7. Identify three words that show that the author set *Hetty Feather* in Victorian times. Think of three replacement words that you would use today.

8. What are the differences between picturing and seeing? Which is real and which is imaginary? Give an example of both in the story.

Focus on...
Purpose, viewpoints and effects

9. Whose viewpoint does the author tell the story from? Which character(s) does the author want you to agree with? Explain your answer.

10. Do you think Hetty is sometimes treated more strictly than the other children with her? Give examples.

11. Are the scenes in this chapter real or is Hetty just picturing them? Can you find an example of both?

12. What is the author's aim in this part of *Hetty Feather*? How does the author achieve this?

Extract 1

- In this extract from the opening pages of the book, Hetty's mother takes her as a baby to be left at the Foundling Hospital.

- Circle 'I' and 'me' in the first paragraph, and 'my' and 'me' in the third paragraph. What do these words indicate about how the book is written? (It is written in the first person.)

- Discuss the author's device of writing the story through the title character. Ask: *How do you think this will affect the reader?* (The reader will see the action from this character's point of view.)

- Underline the final sentence in paragraph two. Discuss why 'can' is in italic font. Ask: *Is it possible to remember what we thought as babies? What does the sentence tell us about Hetty?* (She exaggerates and has a strong imagination.)

- Read aloud paragraph three. Discuss the picture presented and the mother's care. Point out the bathing, dressing and wrapping, and underline 'a little white gown she had stitched herself'. Suggest that such an attentive mother is important to Hetty's supposed memories.

- Circle loud sound verbs and nouns in paragraphs three to five: 'cried', 'shouted' (verbs); 'roar', 'whistle', 'clack', 'bump-clack' (nouns). Circle 'whispered' in the final sentence. Identify it as a soft sound verb that contrasts with the previous harsh loud ones.

- Ask: *Why does the author begin a new paragraph for the final sentence?* (Someone speaks.) Point out the position of punctuation marks, and explain that some authors prefer to use single speech marks, as here.

Extract 2

- This extract is from Chapter 7, and focuses on Hetty's dream about her sneaked visit to the fair and her meeting with Madame Adeline.

- Invite the children to count the paragraphs. Why are there so many? (The text is mainly dialogue.) Point out that the speaker's name is often omitted because a new paragraph makes it obvious who is talking.

- Indicate this sentence: *"I couldn't sleep, Father," I said.* Ask the children to identify spoken and non-spoken words. Circle speech marks, explaining that authors sometimes use single inverted commas rather than double. Circle the second comma. What is its function? (to divide the spoken and non-spoken parts of the sentence) Which punctuation mark divides the sentence before this one? Circle the question mark after 'minx'.

- Give the boys in the class the part of Jem, the girls the part of Hetty. Let them read the dialogue in the first half of the extract. Afterwards, ask them about how they, in character, felt. Discuss what they learn about the characters, particularly Hetty. Comment on her determination, fearlessness and her need for a real mother.

- Give the whole class the part of Hetty as you read Father's dialogue and the children read Hetty's. Ask: *How did you feel when Father said his final words to you?*

- What does Father mean by his final sentence? Point out that Hetty's return to the Foundling Hospital is hanging over her.

Extract 3

- Taken from Chapter 17, this extract describes the scene in London for the celebration of Queen Victoria's Golden Jubilee.

- Read aloud as far as the first comma. Discuss what Hetty means and why she says it. (The Foundling Hospital children were never taken into London, so it would have looked marvellous to them, however poor the visibility.)

- Read the first paragraph aloud. Remind the children that Hetty is the storyteller. Comment on her detailed description of the scene and her precise and educated word selection. Circle 'wondrous', 'palatially', 'embellished', 'loiter', 'craned' and 'marvelling' for the children to supply synonyms. Ask: *Why is 'craned' a powerful verb choice?* (It presents the reader with a strong image of Hetty's stretched neck.)

- Underline 'emporiums'. What are they? (shops) The use of the word reminds the reader of what? (This is a Victorian story.) What word in paragraph two is a similar reminder of the book's time setting? ('omnibuses')

- Circle 'puny' in the second paragraph. Discuss the choice of adjective. Consider how well it contrasts ordinary small, weak policemen with 'so many cabs and carriages and enormous omnibuses'.

- Comment on the detail in the final paragraph's description of the park scene. Which sense is mainly appealed to? (sight) Circle 'freely'. Why does Hetty use this word? Is it the contrast she sees with the restrictive regime of in the Foundling Hospital? Read aloud the final two sentences. Circle 'wonderful'. Ask: *Are the clothes really wonderful or do they just look that way to Hetty because her uniform is so drab?*

Extract 4

- This extract is a non-fiction text about Queen Victoria. It provides information about the celebrations marking her Golden Jubilee.

- Highlight the title. Explain that it indicates what the text is about.

- Underline and read aloud the opening statement. What does it achieve? (It introduces the subject.) Read aloud the second sentence and discuss the first paragraph's function. Point out that having introduced the topic of the Golden Jubilee, the paragraph then answers questions about why and how it was celebrated.

- Question the children about divisions in the remaining text. (paragraphs) Underline the dates heading the three paragraphs. Explain that such subheadings are common in information text. What is their purpose? (They help the reader to access information.)

- Circle 'Victoria', 'Prince Albert', 'Frogmore House', 'Hyde Park', 'Buckingham Palace', 'London'. Emphasise that they name real people and places, essential in a text providing historical information.

- Circle 'landau'. Ask: *What is it?* (A landau is a four-wheeled carriage, usually horse-drawn and with two folding hoods meeting over the middle.) The correct term gives historical authenticity to the text.

- Read paragraph four aloud. Ask: *Which of the extracts is this paragraph similar to? Why?* (Extract 3 also describes the event in Hyde Park.) Point out that the information is briefer and clearer in this non-fiction text. Is this because there is less description?

- Underline 'At the end' in the final sentence. Identify it as a fronted adverbial: a phrase functioning as an adverb and placed in front of the verb. Circle the comma after 'end'. Explain that a comma often follows a fronted adverbial.

Extract 1

Chapter 1

She didn't *want* to give me away. She loved me with all her heart. I know I was a poor, puny little thing, hardly weighing so much as a twist of sugar. I'm sure my mother nursed me night and day, trying her hardest to build me up and make me strong. If I close my eyes now and hunch up small, I can almost feel her arms around me, hear her humming a lullaby, smell her sweet perfume, clasp her white hand with my tiny fingers. I cannot focus properly, but if I try really hard I can see her pale face, the tears in her own blue eyes.

Everyone says you can't remember back to babyhood. I've asked the nurses and the teachers and they all say the same. Even Jem insisted this is true, and he is the wisest boy ever. However, I'm absolutely certain they are all wrong on this point. I *can* remember.

I remember the worst day ever, when my mother bathed me and dressed me in my napkin and my petticoats and a little white gown she had stitched herself. She wrapped me up in a crocheted shawl and then carried me outside. She took me on a long, long journey. I'm sure I remember the roar and whistle of a train. Then I think we took a cab because I cried at the strange bumping and the clack of the horses' hooves. She held me tighter, rocking me in her arms, crying too.

Then the bump-clack stopped and my mother stayed crouching inside, shaking, so that I shook too. The cabman shouted at her and she gave me one last desperate kiss.

'I will always love you,' she whispered right into my ear.

Extract 2

Chapter 7

'You don't understand, Jem,' I said.

'I *know* I don't understand! You really are the limit, Hetty.'

'I *have* to go to the circus. Don't you see?' Madame Adeline is my *mother*!'

'What did you say? Oh, Hetty, really!' He started laughing.

I pummelled him hard. 'Don't laugh at me! It's true. She told me in my dream.'

'Yes, in your *dream*, Hetty. Not really,' said Jem patiently, trying to catch my wrists. 'Stop hitting me!'

'But you have to believe me. It *is* real. We are so alike, Madame Adeline and me.'

'No you're not! Not the slightest little bit.'

'Look at our hair!'

'Hetty, I don't think Madame Adeline's hair is *really* red, not that bright colour. I think she maybe dyes it.'

'*My* hair is bright, and I do not dye mine. We are so totally alike. Take me to the circus and you will see for yourself.'

'I'm not taking you back to the circus.'

'Then I will go by myself.'

'If you try to do that you will get lost. You are too little to find the way. It will kill Mother if she loses another child. And Father will most likely kill *you* if he finds you – and me, into the bargain. Now lie down properly, and go back to sleep like a good little girl.'

He forced me down on my pillow but I couldn't sleep, though I tried hard to seek refuge in my dreams. Eventually I heard Father getting up for work. I slid out of bed quickly and caught him as he went down the stairs.

'Why are you up so early, little minx?' he asked.

'I couldn't sleep, Father,' I said.

'I'm not surprised. I dare say this whole circus escapade was all down to you, Hetty. You have a knack for leading the others astray. Jem's a sensible lad but he's soft as butter where you're concerned.' Father shook his head at me. 'I don't know what to do with you, child. Perhaps it's just as well you won't be with us much longer.'

Extract 3

Chapter 17

London would have looked wondrous to us in a thick fog, but this sparkling, sunny June morning made every great grey building gleam palatially. Every window ledge was decked with bunting, every lamppost embellished with bouquets, every flag flapping in the light breeze. We were told not to break step or loiter even for a second, though I craned my neck and stared when we were marched along Oxford Street, marvelling at the vast emporiums, their windows a wonder of patriotic red, white and blue decoration.

I couldn't get used to the crowds – such huge numbers of people, all shouting, laughing, screaming. Some of our little children started crying in sheer shock, and even I felt frightened, especially when we had to cross a vast road. There were policemen who held up the traffic for us, but they were only puny men. I did not see how they could control so many cabs and carriages and enormous omnibuses. But somehow we all crossed safely, hanging onto each other, our palms sweating.

It was a long, long walk and the little ones in front started dragging their feet and limping in their hard boots, but our spirits picked up as we passed the great Marble Arch and entered the park.

There were ten enormous marquees and many other smaller tents as far as you could see. There were merry-go-rounds and helter-skelters and whirling chairs and swingboats. Children ran around freely everywhere, climbing on the painted horses, sliding down the helter-skelter, squealing with fearful joy in the chairs and boats high above our heads. There were thousands and thousands of children, from tiny tots in pinafores to great girls and boys much taller than me. They were all wearing such wonderful clothes!

Extract 4

The Golden Jubilee

By June 1887, Queen Victoria had reigned on the throne for fifty years. Few British monarchs before her had reached this milestone, so the occasion was celebrated over many days with personal, family, royal and public events.

June 20 1887

The Queen began her anniversary with some quiet reflection at Frogmore House, the royal country residence where her late husband, Prince Albert, was buried. In the evening, she entertained fifty foreign kings and princes, along with governing heads of Britain's overseas colonies and dominions, to a banquet at Buckingham Palace.

June 21 1887

Queen Victoria travelled in an open landau to Westminster Abbey. The route of her procession was lined with terraced benches of onlookers, and dense crowds of spectators beyond. On return to Buckingham Palace, she appeared on the balcony and was cheered by huge crowds of people that had gathered. Inside the Palace, each member of her family was presented with a brooch made for the Jubilee. Later that evening, the Queen was treated to a display of fireworks in the Palace garden.

June 23 1887

By the Queen's decree, a great festival gathering of the school children of London was held in Hyde Park. About 30,000 children and their teachers were fed in the ten huge marquees and numerous smaller ones specially pitched in one section of the Park. In other areas of the Park, there were innumerable attractions, amusements and fairground games for the children's entertainment. At the end, each child was presented with a Jubilee Souvenir Cup to mark the glorious occasion.

GRAMMAR, PUNCTUATION & SPELLING

1. Fronted adverbials

Objective

To use fronted adverbials.

What you need

Copies of *Hetty Feather*, interactive activity 'Fronted adverbials', printable page 'Fronted adverbials'.

What to do

- Complete this activity after reading Chapter 3. Remind the children what an 'adverb' is: a word that adds meaning to the verb. Define 'adverbial': a phrase used instead of an adverb. Explain that an adverbial does not contain a verb.

- Display the interactive activity. Let the children work in pairs to identify the adverbial in each sentence.

- Focus on Screen 6. Remind the children that previous adverbials have followed the verbs. What do they notice in this sentence? (The adverbial precedes the verb.) Introduce the term 'fronted adverbial'; explain that it is an adverbial that is placed before the verb.

- Return to the other screens. The children move the adverbials to make them fronted adverbials and then write their new sentences on their whiteboards. Go through the answers together. As you read the new sentence aloud, the children decide where a comma is needed. Ask: *What have you found out?* (Fronted adverbials are usually separated from the rest of the sentence by a comma.)

- Give out copies of printable page 'Fronted adverbials' for the children to complete.

Differentiation

Support: Offer support when writing the new sentence from the interactive. Explain and complete a sentence on the printable page.
Extension: Ask the children to identify three adverbs on the first two pages of Chapter 3 of *Hetty Feather*. Challenge them to change these into fronted adverbials and to decide on punctuation changes.

2. Making links

Objective

To extend the range of sentences by using a wider range of conjunctions.

What you need

Copies of *Hetty Feather*, photocopiable page 22 'Making links', interactive activity 'Using conjunctions'.

Cross-curricular link

History

What to do

- Complete this activity after reading Chapter 10. On the board write: 'Although Hetty was a new girl, she spoke up for herself.' Identify it as a complex sentence: it has a main clause and a subordinate clause. What joins the clauses? Identify 'although' as a conjunction, a joining word or phrase.

- Display the interactive activity. Read it aloud. Work through the text a paragraph at a time for the children, in pairs, to identify the conjunctions. Ask pairs to give answers to each other before you accept class answers. Click and highlight the agreed conjunctions.

- Ask: *What do you notice about the position of a conjunction?* (It may begin the connected sentence or be in the middle.)

- Give out copies of photocopiable page 22. Check that the children understand what to do. Encourage them to plan their answers before they write any.

- Afterwards, suggest that the children read their answers to a partner. This will help them to 'hear' where commas are needed. Share answers. Point out the variety of the conjunction links.

Differentiation

Support: Let partners work together. Encourage oral preparation. Reduce the conjunction choice.
Extension: Ask the children to review a page of their last story and consider improvements: substituting or moving conjunctions, joining short sentences.

3. Marking speech

Objective

To use direct speech.

What you need

Copies of *Hetty Feather*, photocopiable page 23 'Marking speech', interactive activity 'Marking speech'.

What to do

- Complete this activity after finishing the book. Introduce the term 'inverted commas'. Explain that these are the marks used to show speech within writing. Clarify that inverted commas work in sets and mark the beginning and end of speech.

- Direct the children to appropriate pages in the last chapter of the book. Ask pairs to show each other a set of inverted commas. Which is the first word spoken in each set? Which is the last?

- Ask: *What is strange about the inverted commas in the book?* (This author uses single rather than the usual double inverted commas.)

- Give out copies of photocopiable page 23. Read the text aloud, making the spoken words obvious. Ask the children to insert the missing inverted commas but not to add other punctuation marks at the moment. Remind them to place the inverted commas in front of the first word spoken in a character's speech and after the last.

- Display the interactive activity. Ask for the children's help in adding the speech punctuation.

- Ask: *What do you notice about the layout of the text?* (the large number of paragraphs) *Why are there so many paragraphs?* (A new paragraph is begun for each speaker.)

Differentiation

Support: In pairs, let the children listen to the text more than once.
Extension: Ask the children to add a few lines of dialogue, placing inverted commas correctly.

4. Punctuating direct speech

Objective

To use and punctuate direct speech.

What you need

Copies of *Hetty Feather*, completed copies of photocopiable page 23 'Marking speech', interactive activity 'Punctuating direct speech'.

What to do

- It is best to complete this activity after finishing the book and Activity 3 'Marking speech'.

- Remind the children that inverted commas indicate speech within writing.

- Direct the children to Ida's final piece of speech on the last page of the book. Ask: *Which punctuation mark separates the sentence's spoken and unspoken words?* (a comma) *Is it placed inside or outside the inverted commas?* (inside)

- Explain that spoken and non-spoken words in a sentence are separated by a punctuation mark, usually a comma, question mark or exclamation mark.

- Put the children into pairs and return their completed copies of photocopiable page 23, for them to read together. Suggest that they take turns saying spoken words aloud to each other as they add a question mark, exclamation mark or comma.

- Display the interactive activity. Ask children to help choose punctuation marks. Does everyone agree? Point out that the choice of punctuation may be a matter of writer preference.

Differentiation

Support: Ask the children to underline the spoken words with a coloured pen before they say them to each other. Offer adult support with the use of exclamation marks.
Extension: Ask the children to check their additional sentences from their completed copies of photocopiable page 23 and to add missing punctuation marks.

5. Using prefixes

Objective

To understand how to add a prefix.

What you need

Copies of *Hetty Feather*, printable page 'Prefix cut-out cards', interactive activity 'Using prefixes', printable page 'Adding prefixes', dictionaries.

What to do

- Print and cut out the cards on the printable page 'Prefix cut-out cards' – one of each per child.

- Introduce the term 'prefix' – a group of letters added to the beginning of a word in order to turn it into another word.

- Point out 'certain' at the end of the book: Write 'certain' on the board. Suggest adding the prefix 'un'. What will the new word be? Write up 'uncertain'. Ask: *What has happened to the meaning?* (It now means the opposite.)

- Put the children into pairs with a card each, one 'un' and one 'in'. Write 'sure' on the board. Invite partners to confer before holding up the prefix to make its opposite. Invite a child to place their prefix in front of the root word and the class to read the new word aloud. Write: 'well', 'correct', 'tidy', 'usual', 'dependent', 'popular', 'edible'. Ask the children to use one of their prefix cards to form the antonym (opposite).

- Explain that other prefixes also have negative meanings. Pairs complete the interactive activity. They should say their new words before typing. Pairs explain to each other what the new words mean before copying them into their books and using them in sentences.

Differentiation

Support: Children just list the new words from the interactive activity. They can tick those they understand and consult a dictionary for the others.

Extension: Children can complete the printable page 'Adding prefixes', to extend their vocabulary using negative prefixes.

6. Spelling homophones

Objective

To spell and use homophones.

What you need

Copies of *Hetty Feather*, interactive activity 'Spelling homophones', photocopiable page 24 'Spelling homophones'.

What to do

- It is best to complete this activity after finishing *Hetty Feather*. Write this sentence on the board: 'Everyone <u>knew</u> that the <u>new</u> girl had red hair.' Underline as shown. Ask partners to read the sentence to each other and say what they notice when they listen to the words underlined. (They sound the same.)

- Identify 'knew' and 'new' as homophones: they are pronounced in the same way. Ask the children if they know any other homophones. Use 'for'/'four', 'sun'/'son', 'cereal'/'serial', 'knight'/'night' and 'air'/'heir' in oral sentences for the children to identify, define and spell.

- Show the children the interactive activity. Explain that the words must be sorted into groups of three homophones. Pairs work together to find their answers. Ask volunteers to drag and drop words into place. As each set of homophones is created, ask half the class to read the words aloud. Do the rest hear words that sound the same?

- Refer the children to the book *Hetty Feather*. Discuss the events of Chapter 20. Give out copies of photocopiable page 24. Explain that the children must complete Hetty's letter by writing the correct homophones from the box.

Differentiation

Support: Put the children into pairs and read the letter and the homophones aloud before they write.

Extension: Challenge the children to think of 8 to 10 more pairs of homophones and use them correctly.

Making links

● Choose a conjunction to join each pair of sentences. Remember to use only one capital letter and one full stop in the new sentence. You may use some conjunctions more than once.

> after   although   as   because   but   if   or   so   since   that   where   while

1. The cab reached the hospital. It stopped.

    _____

2. Hetty listened outside the door. She heard no happy children.

    _____

3. Hetty wanted to stay with Gideon. He was only little.

    _____

4. Hetty was nervous. She tried to be brave.

    _____

5. Her old clothes were thrown away. She was given a rough dress and stockings.

    _____

6. Hetty wriggled and squirmed. Matron Peters scrubbed her with carbolic soap.

    _____

7. Hetty's prized possession was a sixpence. Jem had given it to her.

    _____

8. Matron Peters pulled a hairbrush through Hetty's hair. It was no longer tangled.

    _____

9. A girl went to the boys' wing. She was punished.

    _____

Marking speech

- Imagine Hetty and Madame Adeline have the conversation below. Put inverted commas around the words they say. Do not put in any other punctuation marks.

I must stay here shouted Hetty.

No said Madame Adeline, gently.

Why can't I asked Hetty.

There's no room explained Madame Adeline.

But I could sleep in the wagon begged Hetty.

It's unsuitable said Madame Adeline.

I could practise riding with you pleaded Hetty.

You are too old to start learning the tricks said Madame Adeline.

You could help me shouted Hetty.

No, I'm too old exclaimed Madame Adeline.

Then what can I do asked Hetty.

Please go back to school and practise writing your stories begged Madame Adeline

Spelling homophones

● Use the words from the box of homophones below to complete Hetty's letter.

there / their / they're	no / know	write / right	allowed / aloud
wait / weight	might / mite	eye / I	pour / poor
sew / so	plaice / place	Deer / Dear	story / storey
no / know	be / bee	ewe / you	grate / great
reed / read	here / hear	tolled / told	

_____ Miss Smith,

I am happier in this _____ now, because I _____
that Ida is my real mother. She has _____ me all about how
she had to give me up. She had _____ money. She was so
_____.

Thank _____ for sending me your wonderful book. I
can _____ my name in it. I wish I could _____
as well as you. You are _____ clever! I am writing my
_____ and remembering not to _____ fanciful.

I will keep writing in my book. One day I hope to become a
_____ writer like you. My books _____ be
published. Just you _____ and see! I will earn lots of money.
Then Ida and _____ will leave _____ and have a
fine house. We will live _____ together, happily ever after.

I am _____ a visitor on Sunday. Please come.

Your loving friend,

Hetty

1. Finding answers

Objective

To predict what might happen from details stated and implied.

What you need

Copies of *Hetty Feather*, photocopiable page 29 'Questions and answers'.

Cross-curricular link

History

What to do

- Use this activity after reading Chapter 1. When posing the questions below, encourage partner discussion before moving to whole-class exchanges.

- Help the children to scan the chapter. Draw attention to Hetty's birth date and the name 'The Foundling Hospital'. Ask: *Who is telling the story?* (Hetty) *What characters do you notice being mentioned? Who do you think will be important in the rest of the book? Where is the main setting?* (the Foundling Hospital) *Does the setting change?* (Hetty has just arrived at Mother's house.)

- Ask the children to fill in the 'What I know about' section of photocopiable page 29, summarising what they know so far about Hetty, the Foundling Hospital and Mother.

- Suggest that there are many questions unanswered; for example, will Mother keep Hetty?

- Invite the children to think about what might happen in the rest of the book. Ask them to write their predictions at the bottom of the page.

- Share predictions. Suggest the children remember them to see if they are right.

Differentiation

Support: Use partner discussion as a preparation for writing. Call attention to points to focus on.
Extension: Widen the study to include Gideon and Jem. Suggest the children check their predictions at different points in the story, amending as the story progresses.

2. Reading moods

Objective

To draw inferences and justify inferences with evidence.

What you need

Copies of *Hetty Feather*.

Cross-curricular link

History

What to do

- Use this activity after reading Chapter 4.

- With the children's copies of *Hetty Feather* closed, read aloud the description of the children receiving their presents on Christmas Day. Ask: *What mood does the writer create?* Talk about a warm, contented feeling in both Hetty and the reader.

- Investigate together the text further on. Point out Martha's parcel. Does the mood change? (It is a reminder that Martha has gone to the Foundling Hospital.) Point out 'Mother weeping' and Father's 'tear' and 'hoarse' voice. Ask the children to write two or three sentences to describe the mood the writer has created and how.

- Explore further on, pointing out Mother's special attention to and Jem's unusual fuss of Saul. Does the reader sense what will happen? Is the mood more serious? Ask the children to write about their feelings now.

- Point out later evidence of sadness: Jem's red eyes and the words 'didn't seem quite sure enough'. Ask: *Are you worried about Hetty?* Guide the children through the rest of the chapter. Ask them to write two or three sentences to describe the mood by the end of the chapter and how it is created.

Differentiation

Support: Expect only one sentence each time and provide starting words.
Extension: Expect greater exploration of the text supported by appropriate quotations.

PLOT, CHARACTER & SETTING

3. Understanding characters

Objective

To infer characters' feelings from their actions.

What you need

Copies of *Hetty Feather*, photocopiable page 30 'Understanding characters'.

What to do

- Use this activity after reading Chapter 6. Explain that numerous characters have been mentioned. Ask: *Which ones spring to mind?* Use partner discussion for the children to name a character they find appealing. Do they dislike any characters? Why? Share views as a class.

- Let partners discuss how writers can reveal character personalities, for example by character actions, dialogue and comments other characters make. Create a class list of these.

- Suggest that the author often allows readers to form their own opinions, rather than telling them what to think. Refer the children to Hetty's behaviour after seeing the circus show: she 'bellowed, stamping her foot', demanding to see Madame Adeline again. The reader may infer that Hetty is ungrateful and unreasonable.

- Give out copies of photocopiable page 30 'Understanding characters'. Suggest that the children concentrate on one character at a time, working with a partner and searching the text to remind themselves of characteristics. Encourage the children to make their own adjective selection.

- Finally, ask the children to write four new adjectives, one for each character.

Differentiation

Support: Reduce the choice of adjectives, leaving only the most appropriate.
Extension: Ask the children to use the chosen adjectives in a full sketch of one of the characters.

4. Moving on

Objective

To ask questions to improve their understanding of a text.

What you need

Copies of *Hetty Feather*, printable page 'True/False cut-out cards', media resource 'Foundling Hospital', interactive activity 'Moving on'.

What to do

- Prepare enough cards from the printable page so that pairs can have one of each.

- Remind the children that early chapters often ended with hints of Hetty's future return to the Foundling Hospital. Refer to the end of Chapters 1, 2, 3 and 4: discuss how Hetty dreads the move to the Foundling Hospital. In Chapter 10 the move happens.

- Display the media resource showing children at a Foundling Hospital. Discuss what the image suggests about life there.

- Suggest that Chapter 10 is an important and difficult chapter, so it is important to follow events. Help the children to scan the text, a few pages at a time; talk about the setting, characters and action.

- Get pairs to ask each other questions that check understanding. Focus on important points, for example: arrival at the hospital; Mother's goodbye; Hetty's loss (removal of clothes, rag doll); her treatment by adults and children.

- Remind the children of the meanings of 'true' and 'false'. Put the children into pairs and give each pair two cards, one saying 'True', the other saying 'False'.

- Explain the interactive activity. Read statements for pairs to discuss. Let the class hold up answers before agreeing which label to click. Invite children to justify the correct answer with textual reference.

Differentiation

Support: Do further oral work about a double page of the chapter.
Extension: Ask the children to progress to Screen 2 of the interactive activity 'Moving on'.

5. Checking meanings

Objective

To use dictionaries to check the meanings of words that they have read.

What you need

Copies of *Hetty Feather*, interactive activity 'Matching meanings', dictionaries.

Cross-curricular link

History

What to do

- Use this activity after reading Chapter 17. Refer the children to the second page of Chapter 1. What important piece of information is there? (the year of Hetty's birth) Who was the queen then? (Victoria) Point out that vocabulary in the book is often chosen deliberately to suit Victorian times.

- Write these words on the board: 'foundling', 'cab', 'omnibus', 'tippet', 'emporium', 'workhouse'. Explain that they have all been used in Chapter 17.

- Ask the children to copy the list of words, then work to locate them in the text and discuss their likely meanings. Are the words in the dictionary? Ask them to write a brief definition of each.

- Display Screen 1 of the interactive activity. Ask the children to check the words and definitions, and invite them to join the words. How many did they define correctly first time?

- Repeat the exercise with these words from Chapter 10: 'shift', 'sixpence', 'drawers', 'serge', 'privy', 'bade'. Let the children find the words in the text and write down definitions from the dictionary before using Screen 2 of the interactive activity to match Victorian words with their meanings.

Differentiation

Support: Give access to an alphabet line when using a dictionary.
Extension: Ask the children to list six words in Chapter 17 they are unsure of. Encourage them to define each in a single word or short phrase.

6. Fiction and fact

Objective

To identify themes in a wide range of books.

What you need

Copies of *Hetty Feather*, photocopiable page 31 'Fact and fiction (1)', printable page 'Fact and fiction (2)'.

Cross-curricular links

History, geography

What to do

- It is best to use this activity after finishing *Hetty Feather*. Remind the children that books are classified as fiction or non-fiction. Ask them to tell a partner which type of book *Hetty Feather* is and why. Confirm that it is fiction because the characters and events are made-up.

- Suggest that the book also contains non-fiction elements, for example its setting. Ask: *Where is most of the book set?* (the Foundling Hospital) Explain that the Foundling Hospital did exist in Victorian times.

- Remind the children of other real places, people and facts referred to in the story and direct them to references in the text. These include: Oxford Street, Marble Arch and Buckingham Palace (Chapter 17); boys and girls were kept apart at the hospital (Chapter 10).

- Give out copies of photocopiable page 31. Explain that the page contains factual information about Victorian times. Suggest that the children read a piece of factual information carefully before deciding which part of the story it supports.

Differentiation

Support: Read the factual information to the children. Encourage partner work to decide on the related part of the story. Accept chapter or page references and short quotations.
Extension: Children progress to complete printable page 'Fact and fiction (2)'.

PLOT, CHARACTER & SETTING

7. Asking questions

Objective

To ask questions to improve their understanding of a text.

What you need

Copies of *Hetty Feather*, printable page 'Asking questions'.

What to do

- It is best to use this activity after finishing *Hetty Feather*. Explain that *Hetty Feather* is a long book, so it is important that the author leaves the reader feeling satisfied.

- Suggest that the author often provokes questions in the reader's mind. Guide the children through scanning Chapter 17. Ask: *What questions are in your mind by the end of the chapter?* Encourage partner discussion and share some ideas. Write one question on the board, for example: 'Will Hetty and Gideon reach the circus?'

- Give out copies of printable page 'Asking questions' for the children to write their own two questions.

- Scan Chapter 18 with the children. Encourage partner discussion about questions they want answered by the chapter's end. Ask the children to write two questions. Repeat the scanning, thinking, talking and writing process for Chapters 19 and 20.

- Suggest that by the end of the book, most questions should have been answered. Ask the children to write the answers, with book quotations or references. Are any questions unanswered?

- Let the children consider the whole book and any unanswered questions, for example: 'Will Jem and Hetty meet again?' Ask the children to complete the photocopiable page. Ask: *How could Jacqueline Wilson answer these questions now?* (in a sequel)

Differentiation

Support: Accept one question at each stage. Offer guidance with finding answers.
Extension: Expect more questions and specific location of answers.

8. Following structures

Objective

To read books which are structured in different ways.

What you need

Copies of *Hetty Feather*, interactive activity 'Following structures'.

Cross-curricular link

History

What to do

- It is best to use this activity after finishing *Hetty Feather*. Choose a suitable novel, for example *Charlotte's Web*, and read aloud from the opening pages. Agree that the book is written in the third person, the author being outside the story and referring to all characters by name or as 'he' or 'she'.

- Read aloud some early paragraphs from *Hetty Feather*. Ask: *How does the author refer to Hetty?* ('I') *Does this book differ from the other novel?* (*Hetty Feather* is written in the first person, the author taking the part of Hetty and telling her story.)

- Explain that *Hetty Feather* is Hetty's life story so far. Consider the book's organisation. How is it divided? (chapters) Do the children have other suggestions for its structure? Suggest that there could be sections or year headings to correspond to events in Hetty's life.

- Display the interactive activity 'Following structures'. Put the children into pairs to discuss the events listed, find them in the book, and decide on their chronological order.

- Share answers. Invite children to drag and drop the sentences into place.

Differentiation

Support: Support the children in finding the relevant chapter for each event.
Extension: Ask the children to name six other important events in Hetty's life story for a partner to sequence.

Questions and answers

- Fill in what you know and what you still have to learn.
- Then write what you think may happen in the future.

	What I know about...	What I don't yet know about...
Hetty		
The Foundling Hospital		
Mother		

What I predict will happen...

Understanding characters

- Choose two adjectives to describe each character from the selection below. Write them under the character's name. Then add two adjectives of your own for each character.

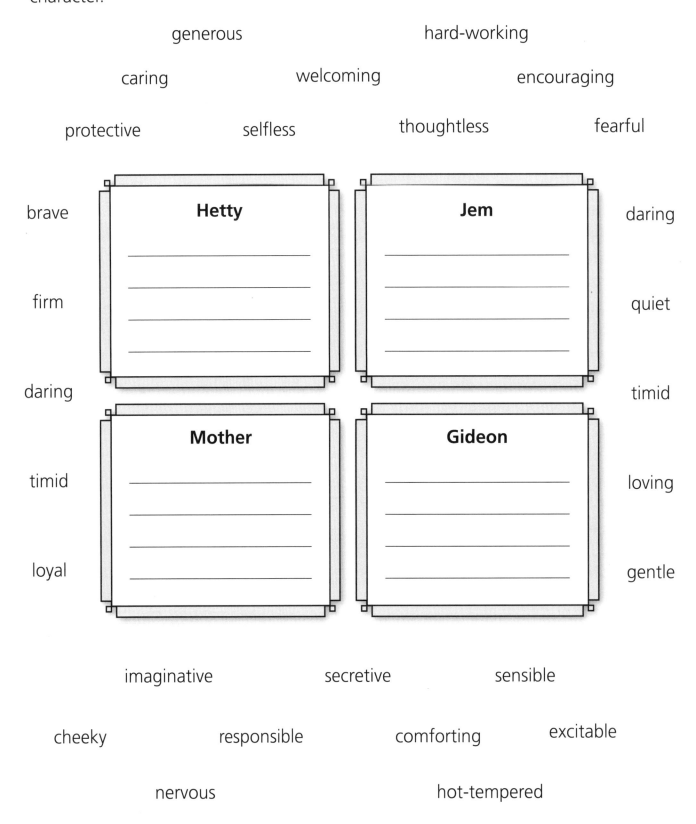

generous

hard-working

caring　　　welcoming　　　encouraging

protective　　　selfless　　　thoughtless　　　fearful

brave
Hetty
daring

firm
_____
_____
_____
_____
quiet

daring
timid

Mother
Gideon

timid
loving

loyal
_____
_____
_____
_____
gentle

imaginative　　　secretive　　　sensible

cheeky　　　responsible　　　comforting　　　excitable

nervous　　　hot-tempered

Fact and fiction (1)

- Find evidence in *Hetty Feather* to support each fact below. Give the chapter number and quote words or describe the event.
- The first one has been done for you.

Fact	Evidence from *Hetty Feather* to support fact
1. In Victorian times, the Foundling Hospital was on Guilford Street in London.	'Please take us to Guilford Street,' said Mother. 'The Foundling Hospital?' said the cab driver. (Chapter 9)
2. Mothers often cut off some hair or a piece of material as a keepsake of their baby.	
3. In the Foundling Hospital, babies were baptised and given a new name. They were never told their original name.	
4. Baby foundlings were sent to be cared for in the countryside by foster mothers until they were about 5 years old.	
5. Queen Victoria's Golden Jubilee included a special celebration in Hyde Park for children, including the foundlings.	

TALK ABOUT IT

1. In the hot seat

To participate in role play.

Copies of *Hetty Feather*.

History

What to do

- Use this activity after reading Chapter 6. Suggest that the reader sometimes wants more detail about characters' feelings and motives than is given explicitly in the text. For example, ask: *Why is Jem so patient with Hetty? How does Father feel about looking after foster children? Does Hetty mind getting into trouble so often?*

- Focus on Hetty. Ask the children, after partner discussion, to agree on and write two questions they would like to ask her. Organise the children into groups of four to compare questions. Ask them to agree on two group questions.

- Explain the term 'hot seat': a role play in which a character is interviewed. Put yourself in the hot seat as Hetty. Turn away and try to make a change to your appearance (add a pair of laced-up boots, for example). Turn and face the class, and invite the groups to ask you their questions, making sure that you answer in role.

- Let groups discuss what they found out about Hetty's personality and motivation. Compare findings as a class.

- Select a different character: Jem, Madame Adeline, Gideon or Saul. Repeat the task as a group activity, one group member taking the hot seat to answer the others' questions.

Support: Provide the children with question starters.
Extension: Ask the children to make close references to the text.

2. Listening to your conscience

To use spoken language to develop understanding through speculating, hypothesising, imagining and exploring ideas.

Copies of *Hetty Feather*.

What to do

- Use this activity after reading Chapter 7. Suggest that the author has made Hetty a mixture of good and bad, for example towards the end of Chapter 7, when Hetty decides to run away from home. Suggest that Hetty might also have thought of obeying Mother and going back to her own bed.

- Divide the class into two groups: Group A represents Hetty's better qualities, while Group B represents her more challenging characteristics. Ask Group A to think of comments to stop Hetty running away. Ask Group B to think of comments to encourage her to run away.

- Organise the two groups into parallel lines facing each other. Take the role of Hetty and walk down the 'alley' between the lines. As you reach children, nod to them to speak their comments. At the end of the alley, having listened to their voices, make your decision.

- Choose children to act as Hetty and repeat the 'conscience alley'. Does each Hetty reach the same decision?

- Try the activity with other situations from the book, for example when Hetty pushes Saul into the pigsty in Chapter 3. Create smaller conscience alleys so that more children experience listening to their conscience.

Support: Provide sample comments and let children speak with a partner in the conscience alley activity.
Extension: Ask children to plan a conscience alley situation for Jem or Mother.

3. Telling a story

Objective

To give well-structured narratives for different purposes, including for expressing feelings.

What you need

Copies of *Hetty Feather*, photocopiable page 35 'A story to tell'.

Cross-curricular link

History

What to do

• Use this activity after reading Chapter 10. Point out that the chapter ends after a difficult 24 hours for many characters. Suggest that Hetty, Mother and Jem had close relationships and all will be thinking about the day. They need to tell their story.

• Guide the children through the main events, starting in the middle of Chapter 8 and finishing at the end of Chapter 10. Point out the unusual fuss made by the family; the dreaded 'hot washing water, though it wasn't bath night'; special cocoa; being dressed in Sunday best; Jem's departure before they get on the train; Mother's goodbye at the hospital.

• Ask the children to decide which character to be: Jem, Hetty or Mother. As storytellers, they must organise their facts in order, describe their feelings and include details, perhaps with information or memories known only to them.

• Give the children photocopiable page 35 and ask them to make notes and sketches, to remind them what happened. Emphasise that they will be *telling*, not reading, their story.

• Let the children practise their storytelling with partners. Organise storytelling groups so everyone experiences speaking to a group.

Differentiation

Support: Suggest doing pictorial and one-word notes for a reduced number of cue cards.
Extension: Ask the children to take the role of Matron Peters.

4. Frozen moments

Objective

To use spoken language to develop understanding through speculating, hypothesising, imagining and exploring ideas.

What you need

Copies of *Hetty Feather*, photocopiable page 36 'Frozen moments'.

What to do

• Use this activity after reading Chapter 12. Explain the term 'freeze-frame' and that in this activity the children will take on the roles of story characters and create a picture of a moment in the story.

• Arrange the children in groups of four. Give each group a card from photocopiable page 36. Ask them to create a freeze-frame for their chosen part of the story.

• Allow 5 to 10 minutes for group discussion and rehearsal. Encourage every member of the group to contribute to decision making.

• Let each group present their freeze-frame to the class. Can the class identify the story moment? Do they recognise the characters? Select individual characters to step out of the tableau and say what they are thinking.

• For other characters in the tableau, encourage the audience to consider what they seem to be thinking. Use thought-tracking, when an audience member stands next to that character and speaks their thoughts aloud.

• Discuss the relevance of facial expression and body language in freeze-frames. Ask the class: *Which expressions and body language helped you with thought-tracking? How?*

Differentiation

Support: Ask children to plan alternative freeze-frames that suggest different character feelings.
Extension: Move among the groups, offering suggestions for poses.

5. Hetty or Sheila?

Objective
To participate in discussions and debates.

What you need
Copies of *Hetty Feather*, photocopiable page 37 'Hetty or Sheila?', media resource 'Hot seat'.

Cross-curricular link
History

What to do
- Direct the children to the early pages of Chapter 17, when Ida chooses Hetty to help her one day then chooses Sheila the next day. Explain that you want the children to consider whether Ida should choose Hetty on the second day.

- Put the children into pairs with a copy of photocopiable page 37. Encourage partner and class discussion of the statements. Point out that some statements may support either case; for example, Hetty has always been Ida's favourite foundling.

- Ask partners to discuss and decide which side to support: having Hetty in the kitchen the next day or choosing someone else. (Make sure there is support for both sides.) The children must choose and cut out the statements they think will support that case.

- Suggest writing notes that list about three arguments supporting having Hetty again or choosing someone else.

- Give yourself the role of chairing the debate and listening to arguments from both sides. Give everyone the chance to speak.

- Finally, sum up what you have heard. Use the media resource 'Hot seat' and read the opinions. Do some children want to change their minds? Ask them to make their final decision and vote.

Differentiation
Support: Children read out the statement they think is the most effective argument.
Extension: Ask the children to argue a third way: having Hetty back for a limited time the next day.

6. Leading characters

Objective
To maintain attention and participate actively in collaborative conversations, staying on topic and initiating and responding to comments.

What you need
Copies of *Hetty Feather*, interactive activity 'Leading characters', printable page 'Leading characters'.

What to do
- Complete this activity after finishing the book. Ask: *Who is the main character? How is this emphasised?* Agree that the title reinforces Hetty's starring role.

- Explain that the children are going to explore the parts played by other characters. Display the interactive activity. Explain that each character has to be paired with the correct description. Put the children into pairs to read the descriptions, discuss the arguments and decide.

- Propose that the author should have used two names in the title: 'Hetty' and one other. Share ideas on how this would have added mystery to the plot. (The reader would have wondered when the character would return, or what would be revealed about them.) Suggest that any of the characters they have just talked about could have been chosen.

- Give out and explain the printable page. Children must match each character to two supporting arguments. At the bottom of the page, they should write their final choice, adding one or two new arguments. Encourage the children to discuss ideas with a partner before writing their choices.

- Share results via group discussions; ask for an oral contribution from everyone. Can the class reach a final choice?

Differentiation
Support: Ask for only one new argument. Give the children a sentence opener when speaking.
Extension: Form new discussion groups, in which everyone supports a different character.

A story to tell

● Write notes to complete the cards below, then use them to help you tell the story from Hetty's, Jem's or Mother's point of view.

Introducing yourself

Who are you?

_____

What did you do differently yesterday evening?

_____

Getting up this morning

How did you feel?

_____

What was strange for you?

_____

Travelling in the cart

How did you try to behave?

_____

What were your thoughts when you saw the station?

_____

Saying goodbye

Did you do it quickly?

_____

What upset you most?

_____

Tonight

What are you thinking and feeling now?

_____

Frozen moments

- Cut out the cards.

Hetty, Mother and Gideon have arrived at the Foundling Hospital. Mother has rung the doorbell. A tall woman with a grim face has opened the door.	Matron Peters questions Hetty about her cut knee. Sheila and Monica are also in the playground, frightened that she will tell Matron that they pushed her over.
Mother is running back towards the cab. At the hospital door, Nurse Beaufort is holding Hetty and Gideon's hands firmly. Hetty calls out, 'Mother!'	Hetty is running back to the girls' wing after visiting Gideon. Some boys are chasing her. Gideon calls out to her and speaks.
Matron Peters takes Hetty to Nurse Winterson's class. Other children in the class are staring, whispering and giggling. Hetty is nervous but angry.	The children are having their Sunday roast. Sunday visitors – ladies and gentlemen – walk around watching the children eat. A gentleman gives Hetty a slab of toffee.
Hetty is in Nurse Winterson's sewing class. She has spotted Martha and thrown her arms around her. Other children laugh. Martha looks worried.	Miss Newman has written a letter on the blackboard. Hetty and the other children are copying it. Hetty is thinking of what she would like to write.

Hetty or Sheila?

- Cut out all the statements. Do you want Ida to choose Hetty tomorrow? Select the statements that support your case.

Hetty is angry because she misses her best friend, Polly.

Hetty has already lost her friend, Polly.

Hetty hurt Ida's feelings by being rude about her job.

Hetty does not want to learn how to be a servant.

Hetty has always been Ida's favourite foundling.

Hetty has had a chance to start learning how to be a cook-general.

▼ GET WRITING

1. A point of view

Objective

To choose pronouns appropriately for clarity and cohesion and to avoid repetition.

What you need

Copies of *Hetty Feather*.

What to do

- Use this activity after reading Chapter 8. Let the children, in pairs, re-read the first page of Chapter 8 and consider the author's writing style. Ask: *Which narrative form is used, third or first person?* (first person) *How can you tell?* ('I' and 'me' are used.) Explain that the author has written the book from the point of view of Hetty, who is recounting her story.

- Discuss what happens in this chapter: the special fuss made of Hetty on her last evening and morning. Identify these lines: 'I opened it carefully and found a silver sixpence… I stared at it in awe.' Ask the children, with a partner, to re-read up to these words the account of Hetty's last evening and morning with the family.

- Suggest that it would be interesting if a different character became 'I' – then the reader could follow the story from a different point of view. Ask the children to become Jem and write his account of what happened that evening and early morning. This way the reader will learn about Jem's feelings. Remind the children to be careful with pronouns: 'I' will now refer to Jem.

Differentiation

Support: Reduce the rewriting to a shorter period of time or to one incident involving Hetty and Jem.
Extension: Ask the children to describe Hetty's last evening and early morning from a different character's point of view.

2. Providing facts

Objective

To write non-narrative material, using simple organisational devices.

What you need

Copies of *Hetty Feather*, Extract 1, printable page 'Non-fiction', printable page 'The Foundling Hospital'.

Cross-curricular link

History

What to do

- Use this activity after reading Chapter 10. Distribute individual copies of Extract 1 and printable page 'Non-fiction'. Read them aloud. Ask pairs to tell each other which is fiction and which is non-fiction.

- Share answers. Agree that Extract 1 is fictional because it is has made-up characters and events; printable page 'Non-fiction' is non-fictional because it informs the reader of facts.

- Suggest that readers of non-fictional texts often search for specific information; they may not want to read from start to finish. Explain that organisational devices can be useful signposts.

- Show the children examples of organisational devices, for example headings and subheadings in a history or science textbook. Demonstrate how they lead the reader to information. Ask the children to improve printable page 'Non-fiction' by adding a heading and four subheadings.

- Give out individual copies of printable page 'The Foundling Hospital', which contains notes about the Foundling Hospital. Children should use the notes to write two new paragraphs, with subheadings, to add to the previous non-fictional text.

Differentiation

Support: Help children to select information to use in one paragraph.
Extension: Ask the children to write a third paragraph.

3. Book review

Objective

To assess the effectiveness of their own and others' writing.

What you need

Copies of *Hetty Feather*, media resource 'Book reviews', photocopiable page 41 'Book review'.

Cross-curricular link

History

What to do

- It is best to complete this activity after finishing *Hetty Feather*. Ask the children to explain to a partner what a book review is. Share ideas and ask: *What are reviews for? Who writes them? Where are they published? Who reads them?*

- Show the children the example book reviews on the media resource 'Book reviews. Explain that there is no set format. Investigate common features: book title, author and, if appropriate, illustrator; story information (without revealing too much of the plot); personal like or dislike of parts of the book; a comment about its suitability for others.

- Hold a class discussion in which the children express their opinions of *Hetty Feather*. Emphasise that their views are not right or wrong – tastes are personal. Encourage the children to support their views with reference to the book. Ask: *What did you particularly enjoy about the book? Where did you think it was most and least successful?*

- Give out individual copies of photocopiable page 41. Children write a review of *Hetty Feather*, writing whole sentences in most sections.

Differentiation

Support: Offer suggestions and encourage discussion when children are deciding what they most liked or disliked about *Hetty Feather*.
Extension: Let the children use their completed photocopiable page as a plan to help them write a polished review for a magazine or website.

4. Creating an ending

Objective

To plan their writing by discussing and recording ideas.

What you need

Copies of *Hetty Feather*, photocopiable page 42 'Creating an ending'.

What to do

- It is best to complete this activity after finishing *Hetty Feather*. Re-read about the last 10 pages of the final chapter, from where Hetty returns to the hospital. Suggest that these pages form the story's ending. Ask: *What is the job of a story's ending?* Compare ideas, agreeing on common features: loose ends can be tied up; plot questions may be answered; plot problems are resolved.

- Identify some of these features in *Hetty Feather*'s ending. Point out that the life of the baby introduced in the first chapter has been followed; the fate of a foundling has been shown; the main character's aim to find her real mother has been fulfilled; the question of why Ida has been so attentive to Hetty has been answered.

- Suggest that the author could have chosen to end the story differently. Let partners tell each other one possible different ending before you share some ideas as a class.

- Set the scenario: Jacqueline Wilson's final section of the book has been lost! The children have to write a new ending. Give out individual copies of photocopiable page 42 for them to make planning notes.

- Let partners discuss their completed plans before, independently, writing their own ending.

Differentiation

Support: Suggest that the children draw pictures of their ending before writing the text.
Extension: Ask the children to plan and talk about a second alternative ending to *Hetty Feather*.

GET WRITING

5. Picture planning

Objective

To draft a narrative, creating settings, characters and plot.

What you need

Copies of *Hetty Feather*.

Cross-curricular link

Art and design

What to do

- Complete this activity after finishing the book. Hold up two books: *Harry Potter and the Philosopher's Stone* and *Harry Potter and the Chamber of Secrets* by J K Rowling. Ask: *What do the titles share?* (the name ('Harry Potter') *Which comes first?* (*Harry Potter and the Philosopher's Stone*) Explain that one book is the sequel to the other: it continues its story.

- Return to *Hetty Feather*. Point out that readers are left with many questions about characters, for example, what will happen to Hetty and Ida.

- Invite partners to share ideas for a sequel to *Hetty Feather*. Ask: *What is the problem?* (Ida and Hetty are poor.) *How do they overcome it?* (Hetty writes her book.) *Who helps them?* (Miss Smith returns.) *What is the ending?*

- Remind them of a story's usual structure of four chronological sections: opening, something happens, events to sort it out, ending. Give each child paper to fold into quarters and number and label with these section headings.

- Invite everyone to create a pictorial storyboard for his or her sequel. Each section may contain more than one picture and should show setting, character and plot. Once completed, save them for the next activity.

Differentiation

Support: Let partners work together on the same story. Provide ideas for one or two sections.
Extension: Ask children to do a second pictorial storyboard.

6. Building a story

Objective

To compose and rehearse sentences orally before writing a text.

What you need

Copies of *Hetty Feather*, photocopiable page 43 'Building a story'.

Cross-curricular link

Art and design

What to do

- Remind the children of Activity 5 'Picture planning', in which they planned a sequel to *Hetty Feather* on a pictorial storyboard.

- Present a storyboard that you have completed for another story. (It should not be related to *Hetty Feather*.) Recount what is happening in each picture.

- Suggest that the next stage in planning is to write notes for each section of the story. Display an enlarged version of photocopiable page 43. Explain that this story planner is useful when making notes.

- Demonstrate writing notes on the photocopiable page. Point out that you are writing words and phrases, not sentences.

- Return to the children's storyboards. Suggest that they remind themselves of their plans by using their storyboard to tell their story to a partner.

- Give out individual copies of photocopiable page. Ask the children to write notes for their sequel.

- Finally, invite the children to write their story in one or more extended writing sessions. Encourage them to take regular pauses to rehearse a sentence orally before writing it.

Differentiation

Support: Let children work with their partners from 'Picture planning', writing only one or two notes for each section.
Extension: Ask the children to add two time conjunctions to each section's notes.

Book review

- Use this sheet to help you write a book review of *Hetty Feather.*

Title _____

Author _____

Illustrator _____

About the story

_____

_____

_____

_____

My favourite part

_____

_____

_____

My least favourite part

_____

_____

_____

Who would enjoy this story?

_____

_____

_____

Now give the book a rating out of five by shading the stars.

☆ ☆ ☆ ☆ ☆

Creating an ending

● Make notes to help you plan a new ending for *Hetty Feather*.

What does Miss Smith tell Matron Bottomly? How does Matron Bottomly react?	
Is Hetty allowed to use her notebook? Does life in the hospital seem just as boring as before?	
How does Ida seem when she sees Hetty again? Has she a new favourite foundling?	
What has happened at the hospital during Hetty's absence? Perhaps someone surprising has turned up.	
Is Hetty left searching for her mother? Maybe her real mother is one of the other characters.	
Is Hetty sad or happy at the end of the book? Could she be thinking of running away again?	
Other ideas I plan to include:	

Building a story

● Use your picture storyboard to help you write planning notes for your story.

1. Opening	●
	●
	●
2. Something happens	●
	●
	●
3. Events to sort it out	●
	●
	●
4. Ending	●
	●
	●

ASSESSMENT

1. Understanding words

To explain the meaning of words in context.

What you need

Copies of *Hetty Feather*, dictionaries.

What to do

- Complete this activity after reading Chapter 10. Write the following sentence on the whiteboard: 'Jem acted in a school play.' Underline 'acted' and ask the children to tell a partner its meaning. Agree a replacement word or phrase to write beside the sentence, for example 'had a role'.

- On the board write: 'Hetty acted foolishly at bedtime.' Underline 'acted' for the children to tell a partner its meaning. Share ideas and agree and write a replacement, for example 'behaved'.

- Ask: *Why is 'acted' defined differently?* (the context changes) Explain that a word may not have always the same meaning. Look up 'act' in a dictionary. Are other meanings suggested?

- Remind the children that *Hetty Feather* is set in Victorian times. The language is often more formal and difficult than that used in a children's book set in modern times.

- List these words on the board: 'extravagantly', 'indignant', 'dormitory', 'tufts', 'plaguing', 'scrawny', 'illuminating', 'remonstrances', 'wretchedly', 'apparel'. Identify them as words from the last four pages of Chapter 10. The children must find each word, copy the phrase containing it, underline the word and write a replacement word or phrase with the same meaning. Emphasise reading the sentence containing the word and using a dictionary well.

Differentiation

Support: Expect fewer completed definitions and accept partner support.
Extension: Let the children repeat the activity with vocabulary from the book's early pages.

2. Possessive apostrophes

Objective

To indicate possession by using the possessive apostrophe with plural nouns.

What you need

Copies of *Hetty Feather*, printable page 'Possessive apostrophes', interactive activity 'Apostrophes'

What to do

- Complete this activity after reading Chapter 10. Say this sentence aloud: 'Hetty has to go to the girls' wing.' Explain that the sentence has two punctuation marks. Ask the children make the marks on their individual whiteboards.

- Ask the children to hold up their whiteboards. They should have marked a full stop and an apostrophe. Ask which word needs the apostrophe and why? ('girls', in order to show ownership) Write the punctuated sentences on the whiteboard. Point out that you are placing the apostrophe after the 's'.

- Explain that the position of a possessive apostrophe is very important. Ask the children to tell you the rules about placing it before or after 's'. Give out and read through printable page 'Possessive apostrophes (1)'. Try applying the tip to your example sentence on the whiteboard.

- Display the interactive activity 'Apostrophes'. Ask the children, in pairs, to decide on each correct option.

- Give out printable page 'Possessive apostrophes (2)', for the children to assess their knowledge. Let them refer to the page of rules.

Differentiation

Support: Let partners prepare their answers to 'Possessive apostrophes (2)' orally before placing the apostrophes.
Extension: Ask the children to identify which rule has been applied each time. Ask them to identify six possessive apostrophes in a recent story they have written.

3. Forming pictures

Objective

To plan their writing by discussing and recording ideas.

What you need

Copies of *Hetty Feather*, photocopiable page 47 'Forming pictures'.

What to do

- Do this activity after reading Chapter 16. Put the children into pairs. When asking questions, be ready to listen in to their answers. Allow time for everyone to speak before accepting any answers from the class.

- Introduce the word 'picturing'. Ask: *What does the author mean by this word?* (the ability to form imaginative mental pictures) *Which character in the book pictures well?* (Hetty) *What does this reveal about Hetty's character?* (She has a powerful imagination.) *How does having the skill of picturing help Hetty?* (It often comforts her by removing her from a harsh reality.)

- Give out individual copies of photocopiable page 47. Explain that three incidents from the book are mentioned on the page. Direct the children to these places in the book and point out the references to picturing. Explain that on each occasion, Hetty uses her picturing skill to change reality to a mental picture that she prefers.

- In pairs, the children read the text describing each incident on the photocopiable page. Ask pairs to discuss Hetty's picturing before they complete the photocopiable page independently. Children should draw in the left-hand box the picture Hetty created, and in the right-hand box describe her thoughts in words.

Differentiation

Support: Read the relevant text to the children before they complete the photocopiable page.
Extension: Challenge the children to find another occasion when Hetty uses her picturing skills?

4. Special people

Objective

To identify themes in a wide range of books.

What you need

Copies of *Hetty Feather*, media resource 'Special people'.

What to do

- Do this activity after reading Chapter 18. Ask the children to re-read the chapter's final two paragraphs. Ask: *What two important decisions has Hetty made?* (to leave Madame Adeline and the hospital) *Why are these decisions so important?* (Hetty is now completely alone.)

- Suggest that Hetty's search to find a special person of her own is the main theme of this book. Ask: *Who does she most want to find?* (her real mother)

- Suggest that at different stages of the story, although always wanting to find her mother, Hetty forms relationships with someone who is special to her. Let partners share ideas about which characters have been special to Hetty. Share some names and talk about when and how these characters have mattered so much to Hetty.

- Display the media resource 'Special people'. Explain that at points in the story each character shown on-screen has fulfilled Hetty's need to find a special person.

- Organise the children into pairs. As you show each image on the media resource, give time for partner discussion before asking the children to write a paragraph independently about the special relationship between Hetty and this character.

Differentiation

Support: Accept simple explanations and more general reference to the text.
Extension: Expect a more detailed answer with closer reference to the text.

5. Discovering facts

Objective

To retrieve and record information from non-fiction.

What you need

Copies of *Hetty Feather*, Extract 4, media resource 'Queen Victoria', reference books.

What to do

- Complete this activity after finishing the book. Let partners discuss answers before you ask: *Who is the queen at the time of this story? What important royal event is in the story?* (Golden Jubilee)

- Guide the children through scanning Chapter 17, picking out references to London, Queen Victoria and her Golden Jubilee. Show the children the picture of the queen in the media resource 'Queen Victoria'.

- Suggest that the Golden Jubilee marks a turning point in the plot. Ask: *Why is the trip to the celebration so important for the story? What is the effect on Hetty?* (Hetty decides to leave the hospital.) Let the children read Chapter 18's final lines and confirm this.

- Distribute copies of Extract 4. Indicate references to Frogmore House and Prince Albert in paragraph 2.

- Appoint the children as newspaper journalists. Their editor wants more detail about Prince Albert (his identity, death); Frogmore House (its location); Victoria's coronation (the date, her age); her widowhood (key changes).

- Provide reference books or internet websites for the children's research. Let the children find the information and write notes in their own words. Keep the children's notes for the next activity.

Differentiation

Support: Let the children research in pairs before writing their own notes.
Extension: Suggest finding out about family members involved in Victoria's Golden Jubilee celebrations.

6. Writing non-fiction

Objective

To draft and write non-narrative material, using simple organisational devices.

What you need

Copies of *Hetty Feather*.

Cross-curricular links

History, computing

What to do

- Talk about Activity 5 'Discovering facts'. Return to the children's notes and remind them of their research areas: Prince Albert; Frogmore House; Victoria's coronation; widowhood.

- Let the children decide on a heading for their report and subheadings for later paragraphs. Suggest that they make a note of these.

- Allow the children to use computers to type a heading for their report and a short paragraph to introduce their subject. This should be followed by subheadings and their remaining paragraphs. Remind the children to use their notes to inform the content of their paragraphs, but to write full sentences.

- When finished, suggest that the children treat their writing as a draft which they then proofread, check, correct, improve and edit. Encourage them to consider spelling, punctuation, the wording of sentences and the organisation of their report.

- Ask them to produce a final version.

Differentiation

Support: Accept less writing and let partners talk to each other about the division of their reports.
Extension: Expect the children to write more and to show more accomplished proofreading and editing skills.

Forming pictures

● Read where each story event occurs. Draw what Hetty pictures is happening. Write an explanation of the picture.

	What Hetty pictures happening	Explanation
In Chapter 10, Hetty's rag doll is taken from her.		
In Chapter 12, Hetty is sitting in the chapel with other foundling girls.		
In Chapter 16, Polly is taken to Matron Bottomly's room.		

SCHOLASTIC

Available in this series:

978-1407-14220-3

978-1407-14219-7

978-1407-14224-1

978-1407-14222-7

978-1407-14223-4

978-1407-15875-4

978-1407-14225-8

978-1407-15877-8

978-1407-14228-9

978-1407-14231-9

978-1407-14226-5 **MAY 2016**

978-1407-14227-2 **MAY 2016**

978-1407-14230-2 **MAY 2016**

978-1407-15876-1 **MAY 2016**

978-1407-15879-2 **MAY 2016**

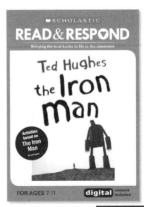

978-1407-14229-6 **MAY 2016**

To find out more, call: 0845 6039091
or visit our website www.scholastic.co.uk/readandrespond